The Usborne
THIRD
Big
Maze
Book

Designed and illustrated by
Ruth Russell, Mattia Cerato, Rob McClurkan,
Lauren Ellis, Candice Whatmore,
Kate Rimmer and Sharon Cooper

Written by Kirsteen Robson

The mazes at the beginning of the
book are easier and they get more
challenging as you go through.
You'll find solutions to all the
mazes on pages 61-64.

Rapid retreat

Quick! Help the mini submarine reverse carefully back to the boat before the slumbering sea monster wakes up.

Supermarket dash

Find Sally a clear route through the town so she can pick up her groceries before the supermarket shuts. The roads sometimes pass under and over each other.

SUPERMARKET

Sally

Gondola ride

How can Marco row his gondola safely along the waterways of Venice to take the tourists to the landing stage? He must avoid other gondolas.

Landing stage

Marco

Car rally

Can you work your way around the rally course in super-quick time to pick up the winner's trophy?

Start here

FINISH

Puffin rock

Perry the puffin has caught a tasty fish, which he wants to share with his friend Penny. Find a route along the rocky ledges that will take him to her. He can hop up or down where there is a step, but he must avoid other puffins, who might steal their supper.

Perry

Penny

Sludge and slime

Which way must the explorers paddle to cross the sludgy swamp without steering into any menacing marsh monsters?

Finish here

Mole-hill hurry

Help Maya Mole make her way through her mole hill and scrabble out into the evening air.

Maya

Croc swamp

Can you lead the rangers back to camp? They must avoid the crocodiles, who will snap at anything that comes too close. The boat can't cross over sandbanks either.

Shake, rattle and roll

Do you dare to travel along the tracks of this spooky roller-coaster ride? Watch out for horrible obstacles and dreadful dead ends.

Skeleton City

Start here

RIP

RIP

RIP

KEEP OUT!

DEAD END

RIP

BOO!

RIP

RIP

The End

Swim, Gloria, swim!

Gloria wants to go home, but which way should she go? She must swim between, not over, the rocks, weeds and shells, keeping close to the sandy seabed.

Home

Gloria

Sugar mice

Can you find a way for Pink Sugar Mouse
to squeeze between the sweet treats
to reach Yellow Sugar Mouse?

Cowboy trail

Jesse has lost his cowboy pals, who have stopped to make camp. Can you discover the trail that will lead him to them? He will need to stop at a watering hole at least once on his way and he can't ride along the same path twice.

Jesse

Finish

Castles in the sand

See if you can wind your way between the sand castles from the blue bucket to the sea, without stepping over any seaweed or starfish. Don't clamber over any crabs either – they may nip your toes.

14

Laboratory labyrinth

Lead Professor Pringle to her Purple Popplemeter before it blows up. She mustn't touch any other equipment, or slip on the spills.

Professor Pringle

Purple Popplemeter

Pony jumps

Paddy and his pony will win the competition
if they can clear only three-bar jumps
all the way to the finish. Find a
prize-winning path for them
across the course.

Paddy

FINISH

Arnie's old car

Arnie has decided to save his old car before it is scrapped.
He has one of its missing wheels but he needs to find two
more on his way. He must hurry to reach
his car, though, before the crane
carries it to the crusher.

Arnie's old car

Arnie

Wolf mountain

Ali needs to take a package to the little blue cottage on his way home over the mountain. Can you guide him safely back to his house so he does not walk in front of any hungry wolves along the way?

Ali

Sizzling sausages

Mmmmm! Patch can smell some spicy sausages sizzling on the barbecue grill. Choose the scent trail that will lead him to lunch.

Patch

Chameleon colony

Sammy the snail has spotted some juicy berries at the top of the bush. Which way should he go to reach them, avoiding the hungry chameleons? He can slide along the stems but he can't jump between branches.

Sammy

Sheep shuffle

Help Sheba the sheepdog round up the straggling sheep and herd them to the rest of the flock in the pen. She can't cross her path or visit any part of the field more than once.

Puddle problem

Felicity is on her way to a party in her new blue shoes.
How can she reach the path without stepping in puddles,
or catching her coat on the soggy tufts of grass?

Felicity

Busy baggage truck

Help the red baggage truck weave its way between the wings to the plane that is being loaded. It mustn't drive over or under anything.

Finish here

Dodge the aliens

This galaxy is swarming with space rocks and alien spacecraft. Which trail must astronaut Eric choose so he can follow Ernie back to planet Earth?

Eric ★

Mini-golf maze

You need six points to win the mini-golf competition.
Can you find a route to a round patch that includes
flags with numbers that add up to six?
You can go under the bridges but
you can't go back on yourself.

2

3

1

1

3

2

1

2

Start
here

Lunar landings

Which set of tracks must Stella steer her space buggy along to pick up her flag-waving assistant? She must avoid rocks and craters.

Stella

Stella's assistant

Seeing the sights

Starting at the Wheel of Wonder, plan the best route to visit all the places listed below (in order) before riding on a river boat. You mustn't take the same road twice.

1. Toyland
2. Café
3. Zoo
4. Fountain
5. Statue
6. Clara's Cakes
7. The Gallery
8. Park

Flag fortress

Two spies from an invading army have climbed the castle walls. How can the spy in the red-flag tower join his fellow spy in the blue-flag tower without pushing past any of the Green Guards along the way?

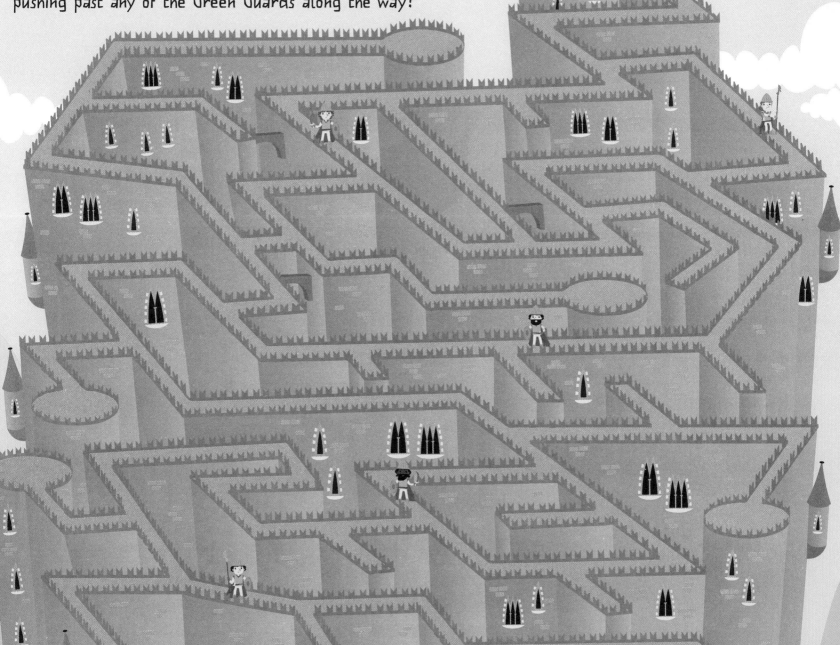

Tiger jungle

Help Herbie back to the lodge. His route might give him a good view of two friendly tigers – see if you can find it.

Herbie

LODGE

Follow the footprints

Phil the wildlife photographer has been searching the woods hoping to find a rare wide-horned spotted deer. He has finally found some tracks. Can you help him trace their owner?

Phil

Pirates' Cove

Find a way down the rocky hillside for the pirates and their plunder. They must stay on the path, or the ponies will stumble. But hurry – the ship will soon set sail!

Pirates

Toy-block town

Which way will you go to the castle?
You mustn't go under any arches, but
you can drive over striped pedestrian
crossings, if the lights are green.

Start

Castle

Band in the park

Rudi is running late for his first concert. Can you help him find the rest of the band and climb onto the stage with his guitar in time for the sound check?

Rudi

Shortcut to the market

Welcome to ancient Rome! When no one is looking, Titus sometimes takes a shortcut through his grandfather's house to the market – but today he's forgotten the way. Can you help him?

Titus

Thirsty friends

Stomp must collect each of his seven friends on his way to the waterhole, so they can follow him there. They mustn't take any path twice. Which way will he go?

Stomp

Snow monsters

Find the path the Arctic adventurer must follow up the icy mountainside to reach the safe house at the top. He must avoid tumbling into ravines or stumbling into snow monsters.

Cycle circuit

The village cycle race ends in the same place as it begins, without taking the same path twice. Which way will the cyclists go?

Start

Finish

Obstacle challenge

Discover a route that will take you to every activity on the obstacle course, going nowhere more than once. Look out for arrows, though – two activities are one-way only.

Start here

Fresh bread!

Help Jacques deliver bread to the door of every beach house with someone inside. He mustn't go the same way twice.

La ville

Jacques

42

Long walk home

You know that you must pass ten dead trees on the long walk home. But where is "home" and how will you get there?

You are here.

Which paths for Peter?

Which perilous paths will lead Peter and Paws to the faraway castle? (They can go over and under bridges, but don't let them walk too close to the edges.)

Peter

Paws

Dairy delivery

The milking is done for the day. Now can you drive the
tractor and trailer along the lanes to Daisy's Dairy?

Daisy's
Dairy

Three peaks trial

To win a medal, the runners have to reach the top of each of the three peaks. They must also stop at two refreshment points along their route. Which path must they follow to finish the race?

Start here

The race ends here.

47

School bus

The yellow bus picks up children at all the stops with odd numbers and the blue bus serves the stops with even numbers. Their routes mustn't cross themselves or each other, or use the same road twice. How will the buses reach the school?

City waterworks

Can you lead Walter the water rat through the puzzling pipes
from the clock tower to the tallest building in the city?
How many ratty friends will he meet on his way?

START

FINISH

Walter

Container yard

Can you lead Don to each container with a red side so he can check the packing notes and finish at the site office? He can't take the same route more than once. Which way will he go?

Don

Site Office

Underground escape

Creep through the castle vaults to escape from the fortress, picking up your treasures on the way. You can't crawl along the same passageway twice and you must gather your treasure in this order:

3x 2x 4x 2x 2x 3x

Circus fun

You are waiting to see the circus. Which path will take you to the Big Top? Hurry, though – the show starts very soon.

WELCOME

Under the arches

Can you make your way around the zoo to meet Paulo for lunch, passing under every arch? You can't walk along the same path twice.

Start here

Paulo

Egyptian explorer

Help the eager explorer find his way
through the snake-infested passages
to discover the hidden tomb of
Pharaoh Phatal the fifth.

Treasure map

The pirates must pick up ten barrels on the way to their buried treasure. Can you plan a route that means they won't sail any stretch of sea more than once?

The pirates are here.

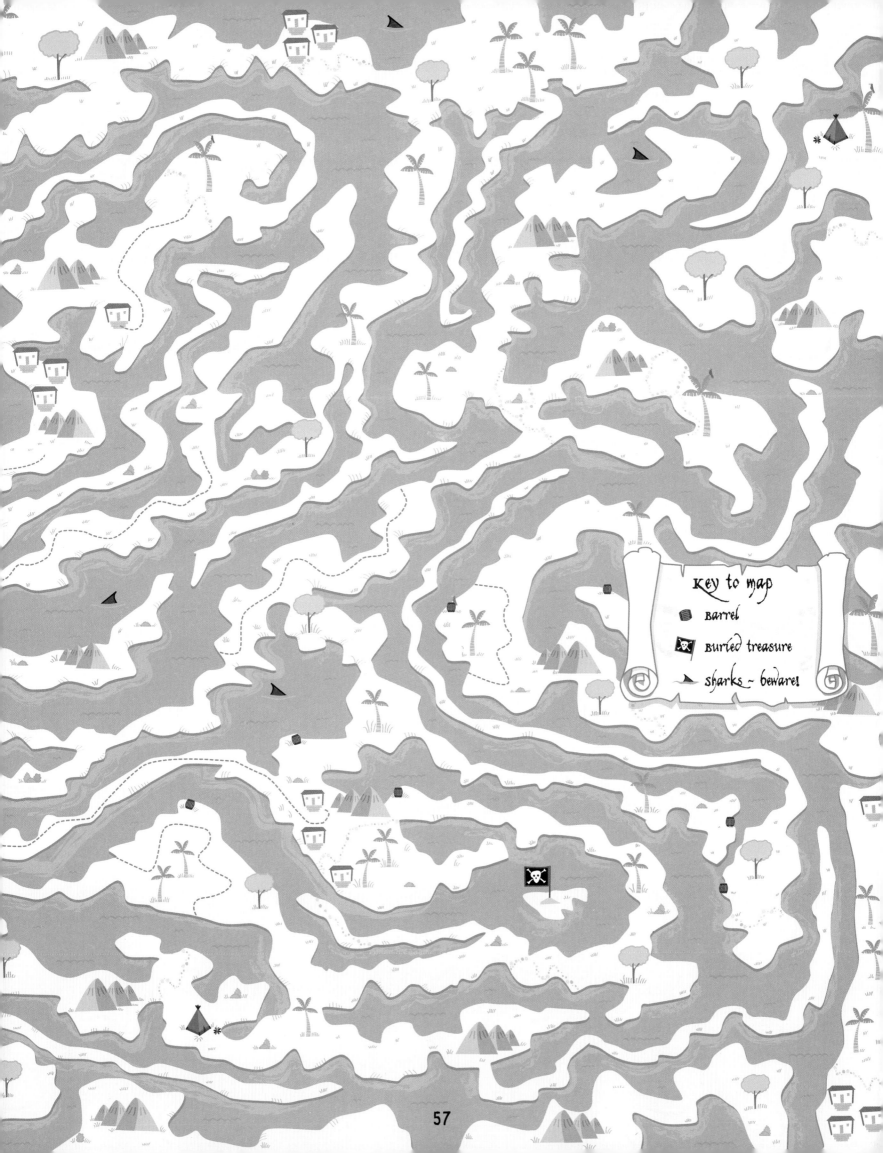

key to map

barrel

buried treasure

sharks ~ beware!

Slide and splash

There's only one way to reach the most popular pool. You can't slide anywhere twice, so which way will you go?

You are here.

Hotdog factory

Which hotdog will be smothered in mustard and which will be covered in ketchup? The tubes twist over and under each other, but the sauce can't pass through the valves on the way.

Mustard

Tomato ketchup

Circuit route

Which route must the electricity zip along to light up the line of bulbs? The electricity can pass through batteries but only green lights, not red.

Start here

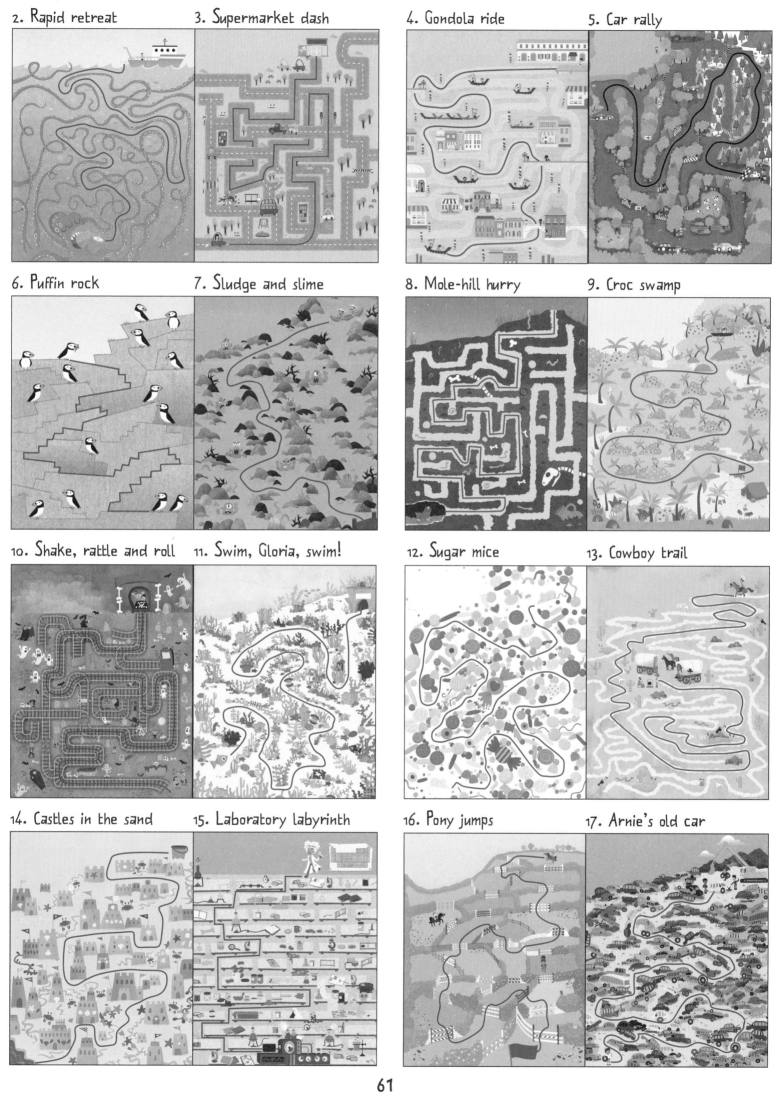

2. Rapid retreat

3. Supermarket dash

4. Gondola ride

5. Car rally

6. Puffin rock

7. Sludge and slime

8. Mole-hill hurry

9. Croc swamp

10. Shake, rattle and roll

11. Swim, Gloria, swim!

12. Sugar mice

13. Cowboy trail

14. Castles in the sand

15. Laboratory labyrinth

16. Pony jumps

17. Arnie's old car

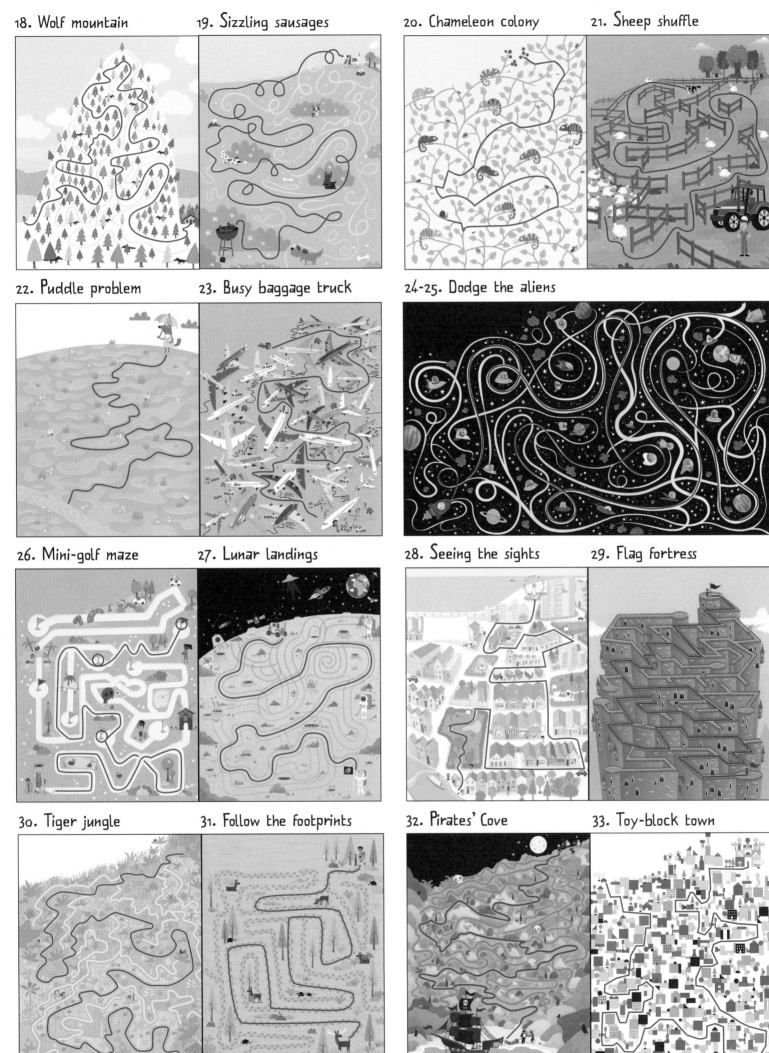

18. Wolf mountain 19. Sizzling sausages 20. Chameleon colony 21. Sheep shuffle

22. Puddle problem 23. Busy baggage truck 24-25. Dodge the aliens

26. Mini-golf maze 27. Lunar landings 28. Seeing the sights 29. Flag fortress

30. Tiger jungle 31. Follow the footprints 32. Pirates' Cove 33. Toy-block town

34-35. Band in the park

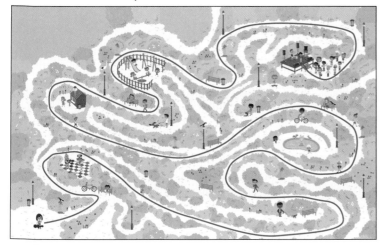

36. Shortcut to the market 37. Thirsty friends

38. Snow monsters   39. Cycle circuit

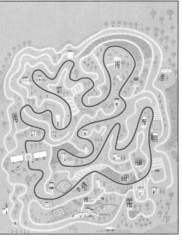

40-41. Obstacle challenge

42. Fresh bread!   43. Long walk home

44. Which paths for Peter? 45. Dairy delivery

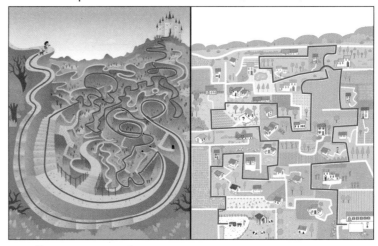

46-47. Three peaks trial

48. School bus   49. City waterworks

4 rats

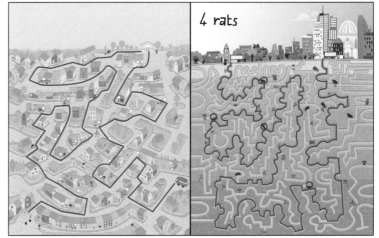

63

50. Container yard 　 51. Underground escape 　 52-53. Circus fun

54. Under the arches 　 55. Egyptian explorer 　 56-57. Treasure map

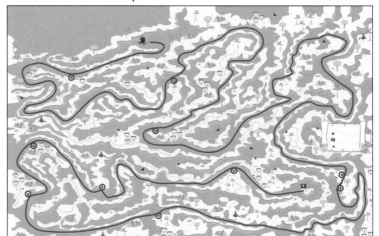

58. Slide and splash 　 59. Hotdog factory 　 60. Circuit route

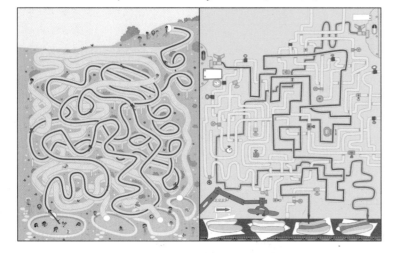
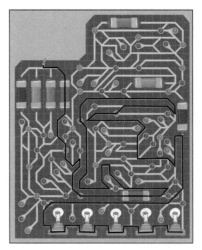

First published in 2015 by Usborne Publishing Ltd. 83–85 Saffron Hill, London ECIN 8RT, England. www.usborne.com
Copyright © 2015 Usborne Publishing Ltd. The name Usborne and the devices ♀♔ are Trade Marks of Usborne Publishing Ltd.
All rights reserved. No part of this publication may be reproduced, stored in a retrieval system, or transmitted in any form or by
any means, electronic, mechanical, photocopying, recording or otherwise, without the prior permission of the publisher.
First published in America in 2015. UE. Printed in Shenzhen, Guangdong, China.